Meditation ☆for Kids☆

Meditation ✧ for Kids ✧

40 Activities to Manage Emotions, Ease Anxiety, and Stay Focused

TEJAL V. PATEL

Illustrations by **Vanessa Boer**

ROCKRIDGE
PRESS

Interior & Cover Designer: Amanda Kirk
Art Producer: Michael Hardgrove
Editor: Lia Ottaviano
Production Editor: Rachel Taenzler

Illustrations © Vanessa Boer, 2020.

Author photo courtesy of
© Alisa Dugan Photography.

ISBN: Print 978-1-64611-532-7
eBook 978-1-64611-845-8

R0

To Rihaan Ohm and Ayaan Aum.

My loves.
My inspiration.
My greatest
spiritual teachers.

CONTENTS

LETTER TO GROWN-UPS

What if meditation was a part of a child's daily routine, along with showering and brushing their teeth? How would it change their life?

That's the question that inspired this book.

In my decade of teaching meditation and mindfulness to children from ages 2 through 8 (including my own), I know for certain that kids CAN meditate (even though they have short attention spans, have endless energy, and rarely sit still). And you don't have to be an expert to teach kids. Because when we teach, we learn, too. I believe meditation should be a family activity, and in this book, I'll teach you and your child simple exercises to strengthen your mindfulness muscle so you can stay present, manage big feelings, and feel calm throughout the day.

Children come into life as joyful beings—let's keep it that way. Meditation has been found to help kids manage their bodies, their energy, their big emotions, and their reaction to stress. Learning how to calm themselves under stress and think of better solutions will not only help them in the present but will also equip them to cope better with life's challenges long term.

Meditation isn't about getting kids to sit still for 10 minutes. It's about teaching them that mental health is just as important as physical health. It's about demonstrating the art of "paying attention" on and off the meditation mat. Most importantly, it's about how to handle the unhappy feelings that are a normal part of life.

Meditation can be explained to kids like this: **Just like we brush our teeth and take a bath to keep our bodies clean, meditation brushes our brains to keep our minds clean from yucky feelings and thoughts. You meditate by taking a peaceful pause in a quiet, safe place so you can rest your mind, reset your mood, and turn on your super powers.**

The 40 exercises in this book, inspired by some of the greatest yogic teachings, will help children combat the most common problems they face on a daily basis—distraction, anger, disappointment, jealousy, and low self-esteem. As you and your child make meditation a part of your daily routines, you will begin to notice positive changes in your overall well-being. You'll focus more, sleep better, stress less, and feel calmer, but most importantly, you will both discover new ways to be present, patient, and peaceful even in the midst of stressful situations.

How to Use This Book:

1. Notice your child's feelings.

2. Find the right chapter.

3. Choose an exercise, read it out loud to your child, and help them follow the steps of the meditation.

Children learn best through imaginative play. That's why each activity is short, fun, and weaves in playfulness to keep kids excited and engaged. And these meditations aren't just for kids—they will help YOU feel less stressed, too. Practice with your child, and you'll be on the right path to building deeper connections, opening communication, and creating a more peaceful home environment.

The Dalai Lama said, **If every eight-year-old in the world is taught meditation, we will eliminate violence from the world within one generation.**

Join me in the revolution to raise the first generation of mindful children and the next generation of peace leaders by sharing pictures of your kids practicing the meditations in this book. Tag me on Instagram, @tejalvpatel, with the hashtag **#kidsCANmeditate**.

For more resources to help you get the most value from this book, go to **www.MeditationForKidsBook.com**.

Let's meditate!

CHAPTER ONE

Rise and Shine

Increase Energy and Set Intentions

Have you ever felt so tired that you just didn't want to get out of bed? Or maybe felt so blah that you wanted to stay inside all day instead? Did you know that how you feel right after you wake up is often how you'll feel for the rest of the day?

Anytime you feel sleepy or sad or your mind feels slow, do a few of these exercises, and you'll feel energized and ready to go. A mindful moment in the morning gives you an energy boost so you can shine your inner light all day.

Zip Up and Sit Up

PEACEFUL PAUSE: Learning to Meditate

Pretend it's a chilly and sunny fall day—better put on your (imaginary) jacket and sunglasses before you go out to play. This is a great way to start the day, and it also gets you in the right position for other meditations in this book. Plus, it's a great bed-itation (meditation you can do in bed) for those mornings when you don't want to get out from under the covers.

1. Sit cross-legged on the floor or bed.

2. Pretend that you are wearing a jacket with a zipper that runs from your belly button to your neck.

3. Sit up tall, grab the pretend zipper, and say **"zzzzziiipp"** out loud as you zip up your jacket. Keep your back nice and straight.

4. Now it's time to put on your sunglasses. Make 2 circles by touching your thumb to your pointer finger on both hands and straighten out the rest of your fingers.

5. Bring your sunglasses up to your eyes and look out as far as you can see.

6. Now rest your sunglasses down on your knees, keeping your back straight. You are zipped up and ready to meditate.

7. Close your eyes and mouth and pretend that you are breathing in a chilly fall breeze through your nose. Then, open your mouth and say **"ahhhhh"** as you breathe out all of that cool air. Breathe in and out like that 3 to 8 more times.

8. Open your eyes, relax your hands, and notice how your body feels.

Take This Time-In When: You are getting your body in the right position to meditate or take a breathing break.

Why It Works: Sitting up with a tall, straight back wakes up your mind and body and allows positive energy to flow.

Yummy or Yucky?

STRESS SCAN: Listening to Your Buttons

Did you know that your body is a machine with special buttons inside? When all your buttons are turned on and working, you'll feel yummy inside. But if any of your buttons are turned off, you'll feel yucky inside. Let's check if all your buttons are working.

1. Zip Up and Sit Up (page 3). Close your eyes.

2. Place your hands on your forehead button. Take a deep breath in and out. Does your head feel yummy like a quiet, starry night sky, or yucky like a loud, howling hurricane wind?

3. Now place your hands on your heart button. Take a deep breath in and out. Does your heart feel yummy like a cold strawberry smoothie, or yucky like hot, heavy lava rocks on your chest?

4. Place your hands on your belly button. Take a deep breath in and out. Does your belly feel yummy like a happy, playful dragon, or yucky like a grumpy, tired dragon?

5. Does any button (head, heart, or belly) feel yucky?

Yucky head means you feel worried. Do Windy Windmill (page 30).

Yucky heart means you feel angry. Try Sippin' Strawberry Smoothies (page 42).

Yucky belly means you feel sad or sleepy. Do Happy Dragon Breaths (page 8).

Take This Time-In When: You don't feel good inside. This scan helps you listen to body sensations, discover where stress lives in your body, what feelings are visiting, and which breathing break will help you feel better.

Why It Works: Stress makes us feel yucky. Listening to sensations like your head feeling loud, your heart feeling hot, or your belly feeling tense helps you know if you are feeling worried, angry, or sad.

Steer Your Ship

MINDFUL MOMENT: Moving through Big Feelings

Often when you feel grumpy, cranky, or whiny, it's because BIG feelings like anger, sadness, fear, or worry are visiting you. But did you know that YOU are in charge of how you feel today? You are the captain of your ship. You control the wheel and can steer your ship to go to any emotion island you want.

1. Zip Up and Sit Up (page 3). Close your eyes and pretend that you are on an island. Which one are you visiting right now: Happy Island, Calm Island, Angry Island, Sad Island, Scared Island, or Tired Island? If you don't like the island you are on right now, you can go to Happy Island or Calm Island instead.

2. Stretch your arms straight in front of you and imagine that you are holding a steering wheel.

3. How many breaths will make you feel better? (Tip: 8 breaths is the magic number.) As you turn your steering wheel to the right, take a deep breath in through your nose. As you turn your steering wheel to the left, take a deep breath out of your nose. Keep steering and breathing until you arrive at your destination and feel calm or happy.

★ **Remember:** You are in charge of how you feel. If you are unhappy, you can hop to a new emotion island any time of day—all you have to do is breathe and steer away.

Take This Time-In When: A big feeling is visiting and you want to feel happy or calm instead. If you feel REALLY upset, settle down and get a hug first before you steer your ship.

Why It Works: It's okay to have BIG feelings. This exercise helps you name feelings and quickly move through BIG feelings when they visit.

Happy Dragon Breaths

BREATHING BREAK: To Boost Your Mood

Sometimes you feel like a grumpy dragon but don't know why. All you have to do to be a happy dragon is blow out all your fire into the sky. Getting rid of your fiery grumpiness will make you feel happy any time of day.

1. When a dragon breathes, its tummy gets really big. Breathe in through your nose to fill your tummy with lots of air.

2. When your tummy is full of air, say **"haaaa"** and breathe out through your mouth to get rid of your fiery feelings and bring your tummy back to normal size.

3. Take another deep breath in, and this time, let out a longer and louder fiery breath.

4. One last time, take a deep breath in and breath out the longest and loudest fire breath through your mouth.

★ **Now all the fire is out and you didn't shout or pout! Enjoy your happy dragon day!**

Take This Time-In When: Your belly feels yucky and you are grumpy because you're tired, bored, or sad. This will get all the grumpies out.

Why It Works: Breathing powerfully out of your mouth releases yucky energy from your body, boosts your mood, and takes away stress.

Launching Rocket Ship

MINDFUL MOVEMENT: Energizing Yoga Pose

It's time to start your day. If you're feeling tired,
let's launch your rocket ship up, up, and away.

1. Stand up straight and tall, spread your legs out wide, and point your feet out to the sides.

2. Now, press your hands together in front of your heart (prayer pose). Slowly squat down as you breathe in for 5 counts: 5 – 4 – 3 – 2 –1 – BLAST OFF!

3. Exhale and explode into the sky. Jump up with your feet together and bring your prayer hands up high above your head.

4. Spread your legs out wide again.

5. Press your hands together in prayer pose in front of your heart. Slowly squat down a little lower than you did the first time as you breathe in for 5 counts: 5 – 4 – 3 – 2 –1 – JUMP!

6. Blast off a little higher this time as you exhale, bring your feet back together, and push your prayer hands straight up in the air.

7. If you still feel tired, you can do it a few more times.

★ **Your energy is now boosted, so have a blast the rest of the day!**

Take This Time-In When: You feel sleepy or lazy and need a quick boost of energy to get moving.

Why It Works: Squatting, jumping up, and bringing your hands above your head are great ways to get energy flowing up your body and into your brain.

Planting Kindness

MINDFUL MOMENT: Sending Kindness to Others

Did you know that every time you do or say something nice to someone, you plant a seed of kindness in their heart? Let's plant some seeds and grow a flower garden of kindness today.

1. Tap on the picture of the seed and think of someone whose heart you want to make happy.

2. Now we must water the seed with kindness. Tap on the watering can, and shower the person with kindness by saying out loud:

> **"May you be safe and healthy.**
>
> **May you feel loved.**
>
> **May you be happy.**
>
> **May you be peaceful."**

3. Tap on the sun and think about how you'll warm the other person's heart when you share your kind wishes with them.

4. Now it's time to go out into the world and watch the garden of kindness grow all around you. Tap on the flower and promise yourself to tell the person your kind wishes when you see them.

5. Repeat steps 1 through 3, this time planting seeds of kindness in your own heart.

Take This Time-In When: You want to feel proud of yourself for sharing your kindness with others.

Why It Works: When we make other people's hearts happy, our heart feels happy, too. Saying nice things to others is a powerful way that you can make the world a kinder, loving, and more compassionate place.

Turn on the Sun Switch

BREATHING BREAK: To Turn up Your Energy

Your nose is like a light switch. If you feel really tired, refuel your energy with this easy breathing exercise.

1. Zip Up and Sit Up (page 3).
2. Straighten your left hand so all your fingers are pointed up to the sky. Take your left thumb and gently close off the left side of your nose.
3. Close your mouth and take a long, slow breath in through the right side of your nose.
4. Then, slowly breathe out through the right side of your nose. Relax your body and feel the warm sun energy flow through you.
5. Repeat 3 to 8 more times. When you're done, press your hands together in front of your heart (prayer pose).
6. Take a deep inhale in as you raise your prayer hands above your head. As you exhale, sweep your arms open around your body to create a beautiful sun around you.

★ Now that your Sun Switch is on, you are energized and fired up to take on the day.

Take This Time-In When: You are cold, tired, or moody and need a boost of energy to get pumped up (especially in the morning).

Why It Works: Your right nostril is connected to the sun energy in your body. When you do right-nostril breathing, it makes your body and mind strong and energized.

Today My Superpower Is . . .

MINDFUL MOMENT: Starting the Day with Positivity

We all have superpowers inside of us. To turn them on, we have to say them out loud. Ready to power up your superpowers?

1. Zip Up and Sit Up (page 3).

2. Pick a superpower from the following list, or make up your own 4-syllable sentence. (Syllables are the chunks that words or sentences are broken up into when we say them out loud. For instance, the sentence "I feel peaceful" has 4 syllables: "I-feel-peace-ful.")

I feel peaceful.

I try my best.

I love myself.

I am happy.

3. Now, let's set your superpower. We'll practice "I feel peaceful." Criss-cross your hands in front of your chest with your palms facing up toward the sky.

4. With both hands at the same time:

> **Touch your thumb to your pointer finger and say "I ."**
> **Touch your thumb to your middle finger and say "Feel."**
> **Touch your thumb to your ring finger and say "Peace."**
> **Touch your thumb to your pinky finger and say "Ful."**

5. Repeat your superpower 2 more times out loud, then 2 more times in a whispering voice, and then 2 more times silently in your mind. Finish by repeating your superpower 2 times in a whisper and 2 times out loud.

6. Raise your hands above your head and shake them out with an excited cheer for 30 seconds.

⭐ Your superpower is set for the day. Power it up anytime by pressing your fingertips together and saying your superpower sentence.

Take This Time-In When: You want to turn on your positivity and self-love superpower. These affirmations will make you feel confident, peaceful, and strong.

Why It Works: Crossing your arms against your chest and touching your fingertips together gives your brain a tune-up and ignites your power.

CHAPTER TWO

Focus Your Mind

Improve Concentration

Has a grown-up ever told you to pay attention, but you just don't know how? Maybe your mind feels too noisy, like there are cars racing around. And no matter how hard you try, your thoughts keep zooming and your mind won't calm down. Whenever you're worried, scared, or nervous, it's tough to concentrate. The exercises in this chapter will help you feel safe, present, and focused.

Meditating on a Lily Pad

MEDITATION: To Feel Safe and Sound

A frog always feels safe and calm when it's sitting on a lily pad in a peaceful lake. Whenever you are having trouble concentrating or feeling calm, just imagine a lily pad of your own and pretend that you are a happy frog, enjoying a moment of peace.

1. Imagine you are a frog sitting on a lily pad.

2. Zip Up and Sit Up (page 3). Close your eyes.

3. Bend your left leg and sit on your left heel. Now, bend your right leg in front of your left leg.

4. Place your frog hands on your heart.

5. When a frog breathes, its tummy gets really, really BIG. Take a deep breath in and fill your tummy with air. Make your tummy BIG - BIG - BIGGER. Then, breathe out and bring your tummy back to normal. Say **"I am safe"** out loud.

6. Breathe in and out and repeat **"I am safe"** four more times.

7. When you are ready, open your eyes and jump off your lily pad. Remember that you are safe anywhere and everywhere you go today.

Take This Time-In When: You feel nervous, worried or scared. Calm down by finding a quiet, peaceful place to rest your mind and remind yourself that you are safe right here, right now.

Why It Works: When you sit on your left heel, it magically sends a message to your brain to stop chatting and be silent. When you place your hand on your heart, it sends the magical message that you have nothing to worry about and it's safe to relax.

Light Up Your Lamp

MINDFUL MOVEMENT: Grounding Yoga Pose

Did you know that the earth has electricity that can charge up your brain?

1. Imagine the ground is an electric socket, your feet are the plug, and your brain is a light bulb in a lamp.

2. Stand up straight. Plug your feet into the socket, pressing them flat on the ground. Raise your arms above your head.

3. Close your eyes. Take a deep breath in and out and imagine the energy from the earth coming into your feet.

4. Now, turn on the light switch. Gently bend your body forward from your hips. Use your finger to touch the ground and press the light switch.

5. Let your arms fall to the floor. Slightly bend your knees and gently nod your head yes and no. Sway your arms from side to side. Dump out your thoughts, worries, and yucky energy from your fingers and head into the ground.

6. Slowly roll back up to a standing position, bring your arms above your head and shake your entire body (arms, head, legs) for 30 seconds.

7. When you're ready to stop shaking, bring your arms to your side, stand still, and breathe. Now your brain is bright and ready to learn.

Take This Time-In When: Your brain feels cloudy and confused. Plant your feet on the ground and breathe in from your feet to light up your brain so creative ideas can flow.

Why It Works: Grounding "plugs" you back into Earth energy, which makes you feel strong and balanced. Bending and shaking moves out yucky energy from your body and mind.

Happy Hummingbird

MINDFUL MOMENT: Humming to Heal

Hummingbirds are always happy because they hum all day. Let's give it a try.

1. Zip Up and Sit Up (page 3) wherever you are.

2. Close your eyes and mouth. Rest your hands on your shoulders to make wings.

3. Imagine you have a long hummingbird beak and you're about to drink nectar from a beautiful flower.

4. Breathe in slowly through your nose. As you breathe out through your nose, keep your mouth closed and make a long and smooth humming sound—**"hummm"**—as you suck up the nectar.

5. As you hum, notice where you feel the humming in your body. Do you feel it in your throat, forehead, or chest?

6. Try it again. Take a deep breath in and **"hummm"** a little louder. Where did you feel the humming this time?

7. Try it again, a little bit softer this time. Take a deep breath in, then breathe out and say **"hummmmm."** Notice how the humming makes your mind feel restful and relaxed.

8. Open your eyes and relax your arms. You are the happiest hummingbird you can be.

Take This Time-In When: You are nervous before a test, you are stressed before a big game, or someone leaves you out of the group or calls you a mean name.

Why It Works: Humming is a powerful exercise that helps you enter your safe, happy place and turn off your freak-out mode (your fight, flight, or freeze response). Humming your favorite song will also quickly shift your mood.

Dolphin Break

MEDITATION: To Empty Your Mind

Sometimes when you think and focus for a really long time, you need a dolphin break to reset your mind and lighten your mood.

1. Imagine that you are a dolphin and you have a hole on the top of your head that you breathe in and out from.

2. Take a slow breath in through the hole. Focus all your attention on your head. As you slowly breathe out, imagine the air flowing out of your tail.

3. To help you focus, use your finger to tap on the dolphin's head on this page. As you breathe in, trace the dolphin's back. As you breathe out, tap on the tail and trace the dolphin's belly back to the head.

4. Take another deep breath in through the top of your head, and let it float all the way down to your legs and feet. As you breathe out, imagine the air flowing out of your dolphin tail.

5. Take 3 to 8 more breaths until your mind feels quiet and calm.

6. Sit still for a moment and notice how your mind feels.

7. Open your eyes. Smile like a playful dolphin and go jump through the waves.

Take This Time-In When: Your mind feels filled to the brim after concentrating or studying for a long time.

Why It Works: Energy goes where your attention flows. When you bring your breath into your head, your mind clears out. When you blow the air out of your feet, you feel grounded.

Stop-Sign Breath

Does your mind ever feel like a noisy, busy city? Like your thoughts are in a big traffic jam and too many cars are racing through your head? When the beeping horns make it hard to focus, be the crossing guard and STOP traffic.

1. Stretch your right hand out in front of you like a big STOP sign.
2. Get the pointer finger of your other hand ready to trace up and down the fingers of your right hand while you take deep breaths.
3. Take a deep breath through your nose as you trace up the first finger.
4. Stop at the top and hold your breath for a moment.
5. Then, trace down your finger slowly while you breathe out of your mouth, saying **"ahhhhh."**
6. Keep tracing up and down all of your fingers, until you have finished tracing your whole hand. When you stop, the city will be calm and the traffic jam will be gone.

Take This Time-In When: You feel hurried, your head hurts, or too many thoughts are racing around your mind. This exercise will help you stop worrying and trust that everything will be fine. Your hands are always with you, so you can stop your thoughts anytime, anywhere.

Why It Works: When you trace your hand slowly and gently, it tells your mind and body that it's safe to get cozy and calm.

Windy Windmill

BREATHING BREAK: To Clear the Mind

Are your thoughts racing fast like a wild hurricane wind, or are they slowly swaying like a summer breeze? Anytime wild, worrying thoughts like "I can't do this" or "What if this happens?" enter your mind, use your windmill to blow them away.

1. Bring both of your pointer fingers in front of your mouth, pointing at each other.

2. Take a deep breath in through your nose for 4 counts, and then blow out through your mouth for 8 counts. As you blow out, spin your pointer fingers around each other as fast as you can, pretending that your breath is a powerful hurricane wind.

3. Repeat step 2, but this time the wind is calmer and the windmill moves slower. Breathe in for 4 counts, then breathe out of your mouth for 8 long counts and slowly circle your fingers.

4. Repeat step 2 again, but this time with a very calm breeze. Take a deep breath in, then breathe out as slowly as you can, circling your fingers very slowly.

5. Continue breathing slowly until your mind is quiet like a starry summer night.

6. Now, you can pick thoughts like "I can do it" and "Even if that happens, I'll be alright."

Take This Time-In When: Your head feels yucky and you need to slow down the racing thoughts.

Why It Works: Making the exhale longer than the inhale sends a message to your mind and body that they can chill out. This breath calms you down by blowing away anxiety and breathing in confidence.

Make a Soul Memory

Did you know your eyes are like cameras? You capture pictures of special moments in your mind and store them in your heart. All you have to do is be mindful, slow down, and focus on what's happening around you—right here, right now. Let's give it a try.

1. Sit completely still and slowly blink your eyes 3 times.

2. Look around you and focus your eyes on something that is not moving.

3. While you stare at the object, take a deep breath in through your nose. Then, as you breathe out through your mouth, whisper **"I am here."**

4. Slowly blink one time and take a picture with your eyes.

5. Look around the picture and practice making a soul memory as you read this book.

6. To keep your memories safe, close your eyes, place your hands on your heart, and take a deep breath in and a deep breath out. Yay! You just made a soul memory that you'll never forget.

Take This Time-In When: There is a moment you don't want to forget (like your birthday party) or you feel bored and need something to do.

Why It Works: This moment will never happen again. Blinking and focusing on an object around you helps you get out of your mind and enjoy the magical moment happening right here, right now.

It's Your Birthday!

MEDITATION: To Boost Happiness

Remember how happy you feel when it's time to blow out the candles on your birthday cake? This birthday cake will help you feel happy any time you feel moody, sad, or mad.

1. Make a wish about how happy you want to feel.
2. Then, take a deep breath in and try to blow out all 5 birthday candles in the picture in one big long breath out. Ready?
   1 - 2 - 3 - Blowwwwww . . .
3. Oh no! They were trick candles. Now, try to blow out all the candles in one big breath again. Ready? 1 - 2 - 3 - Blowwwwww . . .
4. It's time to light your birthday candles again. This time, try to blow out the candles one at a time using quick, short breaths. Ready? Blow - blow - blow - blow - blow.
5. One more time—take a deep breath in and blow out the candles in short, quick breaths: Blow - blow - blow - blow - blow.
6. To finish up, take a long deep breath in through your nose, and breathe out slowly through your nose. Smile and feel happy just like it's your birthday!

Take This Time-In When: Things aren't going your way. Instead of getting upset, do birthday breaths to feel happy instead.

Why It Works: When you take long, deep breaths out of your mouth, you push out sad feelings from your body. When you blow out quick, short breaths from your mouth, it cheers you up quickly so you feel happy again.

CHAPTER THREE

Open Your Heart

Encourage Self-Acceptance, Kindness toward Self and Others, and Connection to the World

Do big feelings visit you when things don't go your way? If so, that's absolutely okay, because grown-ups also feel that way. It's safe to feel all feelings, no matter how positive or negative they might be. Next time a big feeling like anger, impatience, or frustration takes over your mind, open your heart, name the feeling, then practice one of the exercises in this chapter. Before you know it, you'll be in a happy and peaceful place again!

Tap Open Your Heart

MINDFUL MOMENT: Turn on Self-Love

Imagine your heart is a big window. When dark feelings like anger fill your heart, it makes your window dirty. Let's clean your window and unlock it so the bright sunshine and fresh, warm breeze can come in.

1. Zip Up and Sit Up (page 3). Close your eyes.

2. Take a deep breath in and out of your heart.

3. Use your hand to gently wipe your heart clean.

4. Take a deep breath in, then say **"ahhhhh"** as you breathe out of your mouth and get rid of all those dark and dusty feelings.

5. Breathe in and out 2 more times. Now the window is clean, so let's unlock it.

6. Using your 4 fingers on one hand, gently tap on your heart to unlock the window. While you tap, say out loud: **"My heart is open. I love myself. I feel peaceful."** Tap and repeat for as long as you want, until you feel a light, warm breeze come into your heart.

7. Take one last deep breath in and breathe out of your heart. Go out into the world and lead with your heart.

Take This Time-In When: You want to say goodbye to yucky, angry feelings like impatience, frustration, or jealousy.

Why It Works: Tapping points on your body with your fingers (also called the Emotional Freedom Technique) turns off the body's fight-or-flight (stress) response and rewires your brain to think more clearly about a problem.

Anger Washing Machine

MINDFUL MOVEMENT: To Release Anger

Anger can feel heavy and icky like wet, dirty clothes. Let's wash this feeling away.

1. Think about what's making you feel upset right now and say it out loud. Now, pretend that whatever is bothering you is a really dirty shirt or pair of pants.

2. Imagine you are a washing machine that can wash all the icky anger away so you can feel clean and fresh. Throw your pretend clothing inside your imaginary washing machine. Now it's time to become a washing machine and wash anger away.

3. Zip Up and Sit Up (page 3).

4. Grab your shoulders with your hands, with 4 fingers in front of your shoulder and your thumbs in back.

5. Take a powerful deep breath in your nose as you twist your chest and head to the right, and then breathe out of your nose when you twist left. Breathe loudly!

6. Start off twisting slowly side to side. When your body feels ready, twist your washing machine to go faster. Twist gently from side to side 5 to 6 times or until the anger is gone.

7. Stop twisting. Sit up tall with your hands on your knees. Breathe in and out. Now the clothes are clean and the anger is gone, so smile and make it a beautiful day.

Take This Time-In When: You are so annoyed or mad that you want to scream, hit, or shout. Do this exercise to move the heavy energy out.

Why It Works: Twisting your chest opens your heart to allow cool air in, and twisting your body moves anger out of your body so you don't scream or shout.

Sippin' Strawberry Smoothies

BREATHING BREAK: To Cool Down Anger

Can you remember a time when you felt so angry that your face and chest felt hot like fire? Sometimes anger makes us say mean things. Don't worry, anger can make grown-ups feel like this, too. Next time anger comes to visit, don't be afraid. Just sip cold strawberry smoothies to cool down.

1. Imagine you're holding a cold strawberry smoothie with a long, twirly straw in your hand.
2. Now, make an "O" shape with your lips and put the straw in your mouth.
3. Take a long, slow sip through the straw as you inhale. Siiippp.
4. Close your mouth and slowly breathe out through your nose.
5. Take as many sips of the smoothie as you need until anger goes away and you feel joyful and want to go play.

Take This Time-In When: You're scared, your chest feels tense, and you want to feel courageous instead.

Why It Works: When you feel mad, your face and body get hot. To calm down emotional stress, you need to cool down. When you breathe in through your mouth, the cool breath brings more air in so you can think and listen before you talk.

Baby Bird Stretch

MINDFUL MOVEMENT: Heart-Opening Yoga Poses

Imagine you are a baby bird trying to fly for the first time. It's okay to feel scared when you try something new.

1. Before your first flight, stretch out your wings. Sit on your knees and spread out your arms to both sides.

2. Take a strong breath in and flap your wings upward. Take a strong breath out as you flap your wings downward. Keep breathing and flapping until your wings feel nice and strong.

3. Next, place your hands on your knees. As you take a breath in, push your belly and spine forward, opening up your heart and chest.

4. Now, breathe out and press your tummy back, rounding your back. Continue flexing back and forth 8 times as you count out loud.

5. Finally, bring your arms behind your back and clasp your hands together. Pull your hands back, away from your body, to fill your heart with bravery. Take a few breaths in and out.

6. Stand up nice and tall. Close your eyes and spread your arms out to both sides.

7. Say out loud: **"Courage is my superpower."** Now, fearlessly flap your wings and fly!

Take This Time-In When: You're scared, your chest feels tense, and you want to feel courageous instead.

Why It Works: Being scared makes you feel small, tight, and hunched down. Opening up your heart and stretching your spine makes you feel strong and brave.

Heart-to-Heart Hug

PEACEFUL PAUSE: Breathe and Bond

If you ever feel upset but don't feel like talking it out, do this exercise with someone you love.

1. Go to someone you love and say, **"I feel yucky inside. Can I have a heart-to-heart hug?"**

2. Wrap your arms around each other so your hearts touch.

3. Once you are close and connected, take 3 deep, long breaths together as you hug. If it feels good and your heart needs more, continue breathing and hugging for as long as you like. Hugging like this fills your heart with love and makes you feel safe.

4. After you hug, check in to see if you feel better and are ready to talk about your problem.

Take This Time-In When: You feel sad, down, and blue. This will help you feel safe and loved, too.

Why It Works: Big bear hugs with hearts touching let energy and love between 2 people flow without words. It creates a greater connection and bond between both people. If you aren't ready to talk about your problem, hug it out first.

Making Anger Mashed Potatoes

MINDFUL MOVEMENT: To Move through Anger

When someone says something mean to you, do you want to say something mean right back? Anger is like a game of hot potato—when you keep throwing it back and forth, everyone ends up getting burned. There is a better choice: Take a second to breathe, drop the hot potato on the floor, and stop playing the game so nobody ends up getting hurt.

1. Pretend that your anger is a steaming hot baked potato.

2. Take a deep breath, count to 4, and throw it on the floor.

3. Say out loud: **"I'm not playing anger hot potato anymore!"**

4. Stomp the potato with your feet and make mashed potatoes on the ground.

5. Stomp until you're calm again and the anger is nowhere to be found. When you choose to let go of anger, you'll spend your time smiling, playing, and laughing instead.

Take This Time-In When: Someone is mean to you and you feel mad. Instead of letting anger make you say and do unkind things, stomp out the anger before you speak. Remember, if you can't say it nicely, stay silent until you can.

Why It Works: Anger is a game that makes everyone sad, and that's not what we want. Throwing away anger is the best solution for everyone. For a more peaceful world, let's work together to stop playing anger hot potato and make mashed potatoes instead. YOU have the power by starting today and telling all your friends.

Get "Presents"

Have you ever felt impatient or bored while waiting? Imagine someone has surprised you with a present. You're so excited that you want to rip open the wrapping paper—NOW. But before you can open the present, you have to wait a few minutes. If you start to get mad because you don't want to wait, remember that being patient is as easy as counting to 4.

1. Imagine there is a imaginary gift box in front of you. As you trace up the box, breathe in through your nose for 4 counts: 1 - 2 - 3 - 4.

2. As you slowly trace the top of the box with your finger hold your breath for 4 counts.

3. Slowly trace down your imaginary box as you breathe out of your nose for 4 counts.

4. Then, hold the breath out as you trace the bottom of the box for 4 counts.

5. Start with 3 breaths. You did it! You should be so proud of yourself! Waiting isn't so bad when you focus on your breathing rather than the thing you are waiting for.

6. Let's reward your patience. What was the BIG surprise inside the box?

Take This Time-In When: You feel impatient, don't want to wait, and want something NOW. Practice box breathing anywhere, like the doctors office, waiting your turn for the slide, or waiting to get food at a restaurant.

Why It Works: You build patience by getting present and learning how to be in the moment. The best present in life (the gift of peace of mind) comes to those who can wait patiently.

Peace Begins with a Smile

MINDFUL MOMENT: Spread Happiness

Do you ever see people around you who look sad, mad, or stressed? Maybe it's your mommy, daddy, teacher, the cashier at the grocery store, or your best friend. The best thing you can do to help other people feel better is to remember that peace begins with YOU, and all you need to do is smile.

1. Place both hands on your heart, smile, and whisper out loud:
   "Peace begins with me. Peace begins with a smile."

2. Smile a little bigger and say it a little louder:
   "Peace begins with me. Peace begins with a smile."

3. One more time, give your most beautiful smile and say loudly:
   "Peace begins with me! Peace begins with a smile!"

⭐ Your beautiful smile has the power to make the world a kinder place. Remember to look deeply into someone's eyes and give them a smile to brighten their heart and day.

Take This Time-In When: You see someone feeling upset and you want to help them feel better.

Why It Works: Smiling is contagious. It's hard to stay sad or upset when someone gives you a beautiful smile. When someone is mean or grumpy, instead of being mean back, just give them a smile. Smiling puts you in a good mood when you feel sad, too.

CHAPTER FOUR

Explore Your Imagination

Encourage Creativity

Did you know that your imagination holds the answers to all your problems? Everything you see in the world—from airplanes to slime to birthday cake—all started with someone using their imagination and learning from their mistakes. Using your imagination is like making a movie in your mind. But it only turns on if you feel playful, grateful, and peaceful inside. So whenever you feel stuck in a problem with no solution in sight, take a peaceful pause with one of these meditations to turn on your confidence, compassion, and inner light.

Be a Star Listener

PEACEFUL PAUSE: Importance of Silence

In the silence we hear things that we cannot see. Let's practice being a star listener.

1. Shhhhhhhh. Very quietly Zip Up and Sit Up (page 3). Close your eyes.

2. Now, click on your listening ears. Put your thumbs in your ears and spread your other fingers out like stars so you can't hear anything at all. Focus on the sounds inside of you. Can you hear your heart beating fast? The sound of your breath? Is your mind chatting, or is it really quiet instead?

3. Take your stars out of your ears, and now listen to the sounds right around you. What do you hear? Is there a buzzing TV, a fussy baby, text message alerts, a humming heater, or a pet playing?

4. Now, focus on the sounds outside in nature. Listen as far as your ears can go. Do you hear birds, trees, trucks, or the breeze? Shhhh. Be really silent—that's the only way you can hear sounds that are coming from far away.

5. When you're ready, open your eyes. Stay quiet for a little longer and see if you can hear the same things.

★ **Being quiet isn't boring. There is so much we can learn about our world if we listen mindfully.**

Take This Time-In When: Too much noise makes you feel yucky, moody, or distracted.

Why It Works: Sounds affect your mood. When it's loud, it's hard to focus and you can feel stressed. Quiet time keeps your brain and body healthy. Silence helps you hear calming sounds like your breath, birds, and the breeze, which you can't hear when it's noisy.

Lazy River Ride

PEACEFUL PAUSE: Accept What Is Happening
and Go With the Flow

Sometimes things won't go your way. It might not seem fair, but it's really okay.

1. Imagine you are in a boat on a big river.

2. Close your eyes, take a deep breath, and be still for a little.

3. When life is hard you'll feel like your boat is fighting against big crashing rapids. No matter how hard you paddle you can't go in the right direction.

4. When this happens, all you have to do is stop paddling and throw the paddles in the river. Lie back in your boat and say, **"Calm down, go with the flow, take a deep breath nice and slow."** And just breathe.

5. Keep repeating until you feel relaxed. You'll notice that the boat will start flowing in the right direction all by itself, like you're on a lazy river ride.

6. Now, enjoy your lazy river ride and just go with the flow.

7. When you're ready, open your eyes. Isn't life easier when you stop fighting and just go along for the ride?

Take This Time-In When: Things don't seem fair. This will help you relax and handle what's happening without getting upset.

Why It Works: When we force things to happen, we feel stuck. Meditation helps us pause, let go, and go with the flow so life is fun and easy.

Who Do You Want to Be?

PEACEFUL PAUSE: Imagine Who You Will Be

Who do you dream to be someday? Answer the questions below and use your imagination to paint a picture of your future self.

1. What do you love to do when you have free time?

2. How do you want to help others feel? Beautiful, strong, healthy, or kind?

3. Who do you want to be someday? Here are some ideas:

   A teacher who helps others learn to be kind.

   A baker who feeds the community.

   A doctor who helps kids get healthy and strong.

   A firefighter who is so brave.

   An author who sparks imagination.

   A basketball player who inspires people to never give up.

   A hairdresser who loves making others feel beautiful and confident.

   An engineer who solves problems and creates new inventions.

   A singer whose music makes people wanna dance.

4. Close your eyes and picture yourself in the future. You can be anything that you can imagine. Talk about it, draw pictures of it, and dream about it as much as you can. You were born with amazing gifts that are already inside of you. When you dream about helping others, you feel ready to do great things in the world—NOW!

Take This Time-In When: You want to imagine the great things you will do and how you can help others now and in the future.

Why It Works: Your imagination is magical because you can create whatever you want in your head and make it happen in real life. You will become who you dream you can be. DREAM BIG!

Magic Carpet Ride

PEACEFUL PAUSE: Rise above Problems

When something upsets you and big feelings won't leave your mind, find a quiet, safe place away from the problem and let your special magic carpet whisk you away.

1. Close your eyes and imagine the moment that made you feel upset. Now say, **"Magic carpet, please take me for a ride."**

2. Pretend to jump onto your magic carpet, then sit on your knees and zoom high in the sky. Notice how it's so quiet and peaceful up in the sky.

3. Look down at the ground at the moment that was upsetting you. Your problem is so small from way up here, and it's no longer bothering you.

4. Now, the magic carpet is going to take you even higher toward the stars. You're surrounded by darkness and twinkling stars. You let go of your worries. All your problems are gone.

5. Then, you notice a star with your name on it. It holds the solution to your problem. Grab the star and put it inside your heart. Now you're ready to head home.

6. Slowly open your eyes. Now, sit in silence and feel the star inside your heart. It will guide you to a mindful solution to your problem at the right time.

Take This Time-In When: You feel completely confused and don't know how to solve your problem.

Why It Works: Meditation helps your mind rest. When your mind is rested, you can find better solutions and make better choices next time.

Climbing Mistake Mountain

PEACEFUL PAUSE: Build Persistence

Have you ever felt frustrated when you can't do something right? Don't be afraid of mistakes—they only mean that you are trying hard to figure something out and get it right. When you feel like something is too hard, instead of giving up, you can move forward one mistake at a time.

1. It only takes one step to start climbing mistake mountain. When you are having a hard time doing something and start to feel like you just want to give up, say **"I can't do this. YET."** Pretend to take that first step up the mountain.

2. Imagine yourself trying again. Say **"I will try my best,"** and take one more step up the mountain. If you say **"I quit,"** you'll fall back to the start. But keep saying positive things, and you'll get to the top.

3. Now say, **"If I'm stuck, I'll ask for help."** Take another step.

4. You're halfway there! Say **"Keep going. I'm on the right track,"** and take another step.

5. Now, before you take the next step, say **"Oops, I made a mistake. I'll try again."**

6. One more step until you're at the top. Say **"I believe in myself. I'll never stop."** Take the final step up to the top of the mountain.

7. YOU DID IT! Give yourself a loud cheer! **"Hooray!"** Say out loud: **"I'm so proud of myself for not giving up."** You're at the top—what a beautiful view. Always remember that you can do anything you put your mind to.

Take This Time-In When: You feel bad about making a mistake. This practice builds patience and persistence to always try your best and not quit.

Why It Works: Affirmations are positive sentences that train your brain to think positive thoughts. When you try new things you won't get it right the first time. You become great when you believe in yourself, try again, and never give up.

Cozy Crystal Cave

PEACEFUL PAUSE: Setting Intentions

Go to a special cozy crystal cave that was made just for you. This is a place where you can make your dreams come true.

1. Close your eyes and let your body relax.
2. Imagine you are standing in front of a cave with a secret door that only you can open.
3. Now, open the door in your mind and imagine you are stepping inside the cave. Picture a crackling, warm fire in the center of the cave.
4. In front of the fire, picture a fluffy pillow and a warm blanket with your name on it. Imagine that you are snuggling under the blanket and staring up at the cave's ceiling, which is covered with colorful, shiny crystals.
5. Think about something you really want, and make a picture of it in your mind.
6. Tap on the picture of the fire 3 times and say your wish out loud. Believe it will happen and place your wish in the fire.
7. Now it's time to leave your special cave. Your heart feels happy and you know your wish will come true when it's the right time. You can come back to your cozy cave to make a wish anytime you like.

Take This Time-In When: You have a dream or wish that you want to come true.

Why It Works: Believing in your dreams and then letting them go is the fuel to make your dreams happen in real life.

Counting Your Blessings

BEING THANKFUL: For What You Have

Being grateful means taking a mindful moment to say "Thank you" for the amazing things and people in your life. When you start counting your blessings, you'll see you always have enough.

1. Say what you are thankful for out loud with someone you love, or do it anytime you are alone.

   Name 1 PLACE you are thankful for.
   Name 2 HEALTHY FOODS you like that you are thankful for.
   Name 3 PEOPLE who are kind to you that you are thankful for.
   Name 4 STRENGTHS you have that you are thankful for.
   Name 5 THINGS IN NATURE you are thankful for.
   Name ANYTHING you are thankful for right now.

2. Now, do a little happy dance and put on a big smile.

3. Press your hands together in front of your heart (prayer pose) and say, **"The blessings I wish for me, I wish for you, too."**

★ If you can't think of something to be thankful for, be thankful that you woke up today to experience a beautiful day full of adventure and surprises.

Take This Time-In When: You want what someone else has, or you feel like you don't have enough and want more stuff or toys.

Why It Works: Feeling grateful makes you feel like you have enough. Thankfulness invites positive energy into your life and lets more happiness and blessings come to you.

Be the Lighthouse

VISUALIZATION: To Be Your Best Self

Did you know that there is a powerful light inside of you? Shining your light helps you be your best self.

1. Close your eyes. Imagine that there is a lighthouse in your heart shooting out sparkling, beaming light. This light is your inner power. It's all the love in your heart. Your lighthouse is always turned on, but sometimes dark clouds block its light. These dark clouds form when you are scared, shout at others, don't believe in yourself, or keep sad feelings stuck inside.

2. Blow away these clouds by saying out loud, **"I am a shining light of love."**

3. Say that sentence over and over until you feel peaceful. When you feel calm, that means the clouds are gone and your light is shining bright. Your light can be seen in your eyes and your smile, and it can be heard in your kind words.

4. Open your eyes. Remember to be the lighthouse for others to show them the way. When you shine your light brightly, it lets others know that it is okay to shine their lights, too. Spread your light and celebrate it. EVERY. SINGLE. DAY.

Take This Time-In When: You want to shine your light by listening to your heart to find your OWN path, answers, and ideas.

Why It Works: Sharing your light makes the world a more beautiful place. It means sharing the real you, finding your gifts, doing what makes you happy—feeling and spreading love and joy. It means standing up for what is right by making the choices and following the paths that feel right in your heart.

CHAPTER FIVE

Relax and Let Go

Find Calm, Relaxation, and Stillness

Is it hard to turn off your mind when it's time for bed? Do you feel wired instead of tired? Some days are fast and busy. Others are slower and more relaxed. When it's time to go to sleep, taking a peaceful pause is the perfect way to feel calm and relaxed. Just remember, you can feel peaceful whenever you choose.

Butterfly Bed-itation

MINDFUL MOVEMENT: To Relax Your Mind and Body

Sometimes when you've had a super-fun day, even though your body is tired, your mind tricks you into thinking you want to stay up and play. Resting like a butterfly will help you go from wired to tired.

1. Pretend that you are a beautiful butterfly resting on a branch.

2. Lie on your bed with your back down, belly up, and your eyes closed.

3. Bend your knees so the soles of your feet touch together. Rest your arms on the sides of your body with your palms facing up toward the sky.

4. Close your eyes and breathe. Feel the cool air come in through your nose and all the way down to your belly. Feel your belly get big like a balloon when you breathe in. Then, blow it all out of your mouth.

5. Slowly flap both your legs up and down like the wings of a butterfly 5 times to get out your last wiggles from the day.

6. Stop fluttering your legs. Be completely still and say quietly, **"I am peaceful. I am calm. I am turning off my mind so I can rest."**

7. Stay very still. Take a deep breath, then slowly breathe out. You have left all your worries behind. And now, like a calm butterfly, you are ready for bed.

Take This Time-In When: It's time for bed but you have too much energy. It's easier to be still when you release all your worries and wiggles from your body.

Why It Works: Butterfly pose helps you stay still, rest your mind, and release stress from your body and mind so it's easier to listen to stories and fall asleep.

Turn on the Moon Switch

BREATHING BREAK: To Wind Down

Remember how your nose is like a light switch (page 15)? When you feel wild and need to wind down, all you have to do is turn on the Moon Switch.

1. Zip Up and Sit Up (page 3) on your bed.

2. Straighten your right hand so all your fingers are pointed up to the sky. Take your right thumb and gently close off the right side of your nose.

3. Close your mouth and take a long, slow breath in through the left side of your nose.

4. Then, slowly breathe out through the left side of your nose. Relax your body and feel the cool moon energy flow through you.

5. Repeat 3 to 8 times. When you're done, bring your hands together in front of your heart (prayer pose).

6. Take a deep breath in and raise your prayer hands above your head. As you exhale, separate and sweep your arms around the sides of your body to create a beautiful moon around you. Now you are cool and calm like the moon.

Take This Time-In When: You are overexcited and want to chill out.

Why It Works: The left side of your nose is connected to the moon energy in your body. Left-nostril breathing helps you unwind anytime (it's not just for bedtime).

Retrace Today's Treasure Map

MINDFUL MOMENT: Reflect on Your Day

Each day is different from every other day. Today will never ever happen the same exact way again. Take out today's treasure map and retrace your adventures. You can do this exercise on your own or with someone you love.

1. Tap on the emotion island you started on this morning, then tap on any other emotion islands you visited today.

2. Touch the top of the mountain and imagine or talk about the best part of your day.

3. Touch the bottom of the ocean and imagine or talk about the lowest part of the day.

4. Touch the sun and think of something that happened today that warmed your heart. Did someone do something nice for you?

5. Touch the flower if you planted kindness in someone else's heart.

6. Now that the moon is on the rise and the sun is about to set, tap on the emotion island where you will dock your ship to rest.

★ **I hope you have the sweetest dreams. Peace to all. Light to all. Love and blessings to all. Namaste.**

Take This Time-In When: You want to have a positive end to your day by feeling grateful for all the fun, feelings, and things you experienced.

Why It Works: Reflecting on your feelings and highs and lows from the day trains your brain to feel grateful, present, and learn from your mistakes.

Sleepy Sea Turtle

MINDFUL MOMENT: Calming Yoga Pose

Anytime your mind is too active when it's time for bed, become a sleepy sea turtle! It will help your mind turn off so you can rest.

1. Sit back on your heels on the floor or your bed.
2. Slowly bring your forehead down to touch the floor in front of your knees.
3. Now stretch and straighten your arms out in front of you with your palms flat on the floor.
4. Close your eyes and relax.
5. Take 8 deep breaths in and out. The sleepy sea turtle is resting in the sand.
6. Now it's your turn to tuck into bed. Sweet dreams and good night.

Take This Time-In When: It's time for bed but you have too much energy.

Why It Works: Child's pose helps your body and mind relax and let go of stress so it's easier to listen to stories and fall asleep.

Peaceful Night Song

RELAXATION: Song Written by Kajal Desai

It's time to go to bed and turn off the lights. Snuggle close to someone you love—now you're ready to wind down and sleep.

1. Sing this song together to the tune of "Silent Night."

   Breathe in. Breathe out.

   Take deep breaths and let it all out.

   Watch my thoughts just fly away.

   Feeling peaceful at the end of the day.

   Go to bed feeling grateful.

   Go to bed feeling loved.

2. Take a deep breath in through your nose, then let it all out.

3. Hug your loved one and say good night. You are off to have a peaceful night.

Take This Time-In When: You want to share a special, snuggly, mindful bedtime moment with someone you love.

Why It Works: Curling up close and hugging before bed makes you feel safe, loved, and deeply connected, which will help you have a good night's sleep.

Let's Start Again . . .

Did you make a mistake today? Don't feel bad if you did. Mistakes can happen every day. Did you say something mean that hurt someone's heart? Did you do something you wish you hadn't done?

1. Think about a mistake you made today. Imagine a button in your mind that says "Start Again," and push it.

2. Now, say out loud, **"I will start again."**

3. Imagine you are putting on your solution-seeker hat. It's safe to talk about what happened with a grown-up you trust. What can you do better next time? Do you want to say sorry to someone?

4. Practice role-playing what you will say and do next time. It's okay to make mistakes. Grown-ups make mistakes, too. Find new solutions and try your best next time around. Remember, every moment is brand new, so you can always **start again.**

Take This Time-In When: You are trying to learn from a mistake. Instead of thinking you are bad, use mistakes as an opportunity to forgive yourself, apologize, and make kinder choices.

Why It Works: Starting again reminds us that at any moment we can make a better choice. When we know better, we can do better.

Face Bath

MINDFUL MOMENT: Relax the Mind Before Bed

Just like a warm bath before bedtime helps your body relax, this face bath will help your mind feel calm and ready for sleep.

1. Zip Up and Sit Up (page 3) on your bed. Rub your hands together and pretend you are getting them all soapy.

2. When your hands feel warm, put them over your eyes. Take a long breath in, then let it all out. Notice how your warm hands feel on your eyes.

3. Rub your hands together a little faster this time, making some energy. Put your hands over your cheeks and let the warmth of your hands soak into your face. Take a long, slow breath in, and then let it all out.

4. Rub your hands together even faster. When your hands feel hot, place them on top of your head and let all the energy flow into your mind.

5. Take a long, slow breath in, and then let it all out. Pause for a moment to notice how peaceful your mind and face feel. Now your mind is relaxed and ready for bed.

Take This Time-In When: Your mind won't shut off before bed.

Why It Works: Your hands are very powerful. You have energy centers in your hands called chakras that get turned on when you rub your hands together until they get hot. Placing warm hands anywhere on your face or body sends a message to your brain that it's safe to relax.

You Are a Gift to the World

Snuggle in bed under a warm blanket, and have someone you love read this to you before you go to sleep.

1. Close your eyes and get comfortable in your bed. Lie down on your back, with a warm blanket on top.

2. Take in a deep breath, and when you let it out, feel everything around you getting calmer and quieter.

3. Imagine there is a big TV screen that is playing a movie all about your life.

4. You see a moment when you did something kind for someone and how you made their heart happy. Think about how good it feels to make someone smile.

5. Now remember a time when someone was kind to you. Think about how great you felt.

6. Let those good feelings warm your heart. These beautiful things happened to you because you are a loving and peaceful soul. Love is about taking care of yourself and other people everyday.

7. Take a nice deep breath in and slowly breathe out. Feel all the wonderful feelings of love and gentleness as you snuggle in for sleep tonight.

★ You are a once-in-a-lifetime miracle. You matter. You are important. You are so loved. Just the way you are. And never forget, you are a gift to the world.

Take This Time-In When: You want to spend time with a loved one at the end of the day.

Why It Works: Knowing how loved you are builds compassion for yourself and others. Every person is loved and special just like you.

HOW TO LEARN MORE ABOUT MEDITATION

Getting Started, Ages 2 And Up

☆ Mindful Moments for Kids by Kira Willey. On Amazon Music, Apple Music, or Spotify.
The best way to introduce meditation and mindful breathing is listening to short guided meditations in the car and during playtime when children are in a good mood.

☆ Breathe, Think, Do with Sesame. On the App Store or Google Play.
This app is intended for parents and caregivers to use with their young children (2 to 5) to help teach skills like deep breathing, problem solving, and self-control.

Resources For Kids Ages 4 And Up

☆ Peaceful Piggy Meditation by Kerry Lee MacLean. Albert Whitman Prairie Books, 2004.
This book is a wonderful introduction to meditation for children and explains how meditation helps peacefully handle tough problems.

☆ Listening to My Body by Gabi Garcia. Skinned Knee Publishing, 2017.
This book helps kids learn how to self-regulate by noticing and naming feelings and sensations. It gives simple practices to help kids be aware of their bodies.

☆ **Meditation for Kids** by Sada. On Amazon Music, Apple Music, or Spotify.

Simple 3- to 5-minute guided meditations you can play at bedtime to help both you and your child relax at the end of the day.

☆ **Love Powered Littles.**

LovePoweredCo.com has amazing affirmation card decks that help kids (and parents) connect to their daily "powers." It builds positive self-talk, self-love, confidence, and connects us to our higher self.

☆ **Stop, Breathe & Think.** On the App Store or Google Play.

This app offers children a fun and easy way to identify emotions from counting breaths to friendly wishes. Each activity brings fun rewards to keep them engaged.

☆ **CosmicKids.com.**

This is a great resource with meditation, yoga, and mindfulness videos for kids to watch and follow along.

☆ **Tejalvpatel.com/how-do-i-teach-mindfulness-to-my-kids/.**

My website has more tips on teaching meditation and mindfulness to young kids ages 3 through 8.

INDEX

ACKNOWLEDGMENTS

The biggest shout-out goes to my old-soul bestie, my four-year-old son, Ayaan Aum. Every exercise in this book is tested, fine-tuned, and approved by him. It's his magical touch that shaped each activity that will get kids excited to meditate and make breathing breaks, yoga, and meditation a norm in many homes.

Big thanks to my friend and fellow mindful mama, Kajal Desai, for contributing your magical "Peaceful Night" song to this book. The book wouldn't be complete without it.

Infinite love and gratitude to my husband, Chirag. You are forever my number one cheerleader and best friend. This dream wouldn't have been possible without you believing in me.

Finally, I thank YOU, my reader. I'm so deeply inspired by your willingness to empower our youth with the tools of mindfulness and meditation. And to every child who meditates with this book, you are my biggest inspiration, purpose, and joy.

☆ ABOUT THE AUTHOR ☆

Tejal V. Patel is a former divorce attorney turned mindfulness and meditation advocate for moms and kids.

Named a "Well-Being Warrior" in the Huffington Post, Tejal's soulful wisdom reaches moms globally through her signature online courses (Mindful Kids Masterclass, Mindful Mama Experience, and 7 Day Stress Detox), inspiring podcast, booming Instagram community, motivating Tejal TV episodes, powerful live events, and laser-sharp coaching.

Her fun and practical ways to infuse mindfulness and meditation into every day makes her a go-to resource for modern moms seeking to raise calm, confident, and compassionate children.

It's Tejal's mission to support moms on their journey to become mindful parents and raise mindful children, too.

Visit **www.MeditationForKidsBook.com** for more resources on how to get the most value from this book.

Get mindful parenting tips and course info at **TejalVPatel.com**.

Connect on Instagram: **@tejalvpatel**.

Tune into her weekly Time-In Talks podcast, in which she talks about the biggest problems modern moms (and kids) face and the spiritual solutions to solve them.

CPSIA information can be obtained
at www.ICGtesting.com
Printed in the USA
BVHW020043080221
599565BV00001B/1

9 781646 115327